T0086294

S.T.O.P!

Look Listen and Learn

CHRISTINE BROOKS

authorHOUSE®

AuthorHouse™
1663 Liberty Drive
Bloomington, IN 47403
www.authorhouse.com
Phone: 1 (800) 839-8640

Published by AuthorHouse 11/02/2016

ISBN: 978-1-5246-4668-4 (sc)
ISBN: 978-1-5246-4667-7 (e)

Library of Congress Control Number: 2016917700

Print information available on the last page.

Any people depicted in stock imagery provided by Thinkstock are models, and such images are being used for illustrative purposes only. Certain stock imagery © Thinkstock.

This book is printed on acid-free paper.

If you don't want to make a change in life and become a better person do not read this book.

I dedicate this book to people

who will never be forgotten

Many people want to be flattered by others, they really don't want to hear the truth about themselves. For example you're a very mean and nasty individual, filled with envy, bitterness, malice, strife hatred and all the works of the flesh. If you can deal with the truth and be real about it, this book is for you.

I was one of these persons, when I was told the truth about myself, I wasn't shocked. I knew it all along. I just did not know how to get rid of it. For years I hid from the individual who told me the truth about myself. However in secret I kept praying and asking God to deliver me from these things and help me to have love for my enemies. Oh yes if you've ever heard about a Mad Black Woman this is exactly who I was, however I was desperate for a change, a real change from the inside out. I had problems and I had real deep issues from childhood

growing up, however some people's issues are greater than others. I prayed and I fasted and I did everything under the sun because I was desperate and I knew if something was not done I don't know where I would end up. I would read the scripture about the fruits of the spirit being love, joy, peace, meekness, kindness, gentleness, temperance etc but I just could not produce them. The scripture also states that you shall know them by their fruit's and I just was not producing the right fruits. The secret was time, I did not know that some people

can produce their fruits easily but some people must study and work at it. Study to show yourself approved a workman that needed not be ashamed rightly dividing the word of truth (I'm paraphrasing) you can look it up in the concordance. Therefore I studied, prayed and fasted.

Today I can say, years ago whenever someone saw me on the street they were liable to walk on the other side of the street because they were not sure if I would hit them because of the bitterness and hostility I had inside of me. Don't get me wrong, I'm not perfect, and I slip

up at times but for the most part I can be approachable and I can be friendly and most of all I can love even my worst enemy and I can be merciful. And by the way if someone professes to be a Christian for years and years and studies the word and fasts and prays with no change at all, something is very wrong with that picture because studying the word of God always brings about a change in a positive direction. They don't have to be perfect but they must change.

You see it all begins with the heart. The heart is deceitful and desperately wicked

who can know it. Only God knows the heart. A person can do everything right but if the heart isn't right they might as well not do anything at all. Even King David who is a man after Gods own heart had murder in his heart. So then how does an individual get to the point where there is perfect love in their heart? The bible states guard the heart with all diligence for out of it flows the issues of life.

If you have ought against your brother or sister put your gift down at the altar and make it right with them before you

give your gift. How can you say you love God whom you have never seen and you hate your brother or your sister whom you can see, God calls you a liar.

I once had a situation in my life where there was favoritism in my family. It was so obvious that my brother was the favourite and I was the out cast. I was upset about the situation and if I can be honest I would say I had hatred and bitterness living inside of me. Someone told me they had the same situation growing up, so I asked them how did you overcome this hurdle? They said I

let them love whoever they wanted to love but I kept on loving them. I took their advice and it worked. I was treated like an outcast but I kept on loving and this is how I got my victory.

You see it's a matter of hitting rock bottom when you realize that you are desperately in need of help. There are many people in the bible who prayed desperate prayers. Hannah for example prayed a desperate prayer. If thou would'st look upon the affliction of thine hand maid and will grant a male child I will give him to you all the days of his life. The

Prophet Elisha also prayed a desperate prayer when those children teased him and called him bald. He called on God to send a bear to eat everyone of them. My question to you is how desperate are you for change or have you become comfortable in your situation and are you just going with the flow. The woman with the issue of blood was so desperate she didn't even pray, maybe she had been praying for years with no change, I don't know however she extended her faith to go a little further and touch the Lord. This could be the case for you, you've

been praying for years with no results then reach out and touch the Master.

There are many people who had major issue in the bible, the man at the pool at Bethsada who sat waiting for the angel to come so that he could be healed, probably had many questions. Lord why did my family and friends desert me and leave me knowing that I am a cripple and I have no one to put me in the pool when the angel comes and the water is troubled. However Jesus himself made a special trip to the pool and answered his request. His question was wilt thou

be made whole? and He said rise take up thy bed and walk and immediately he was healed. The man had to be desperate, first of all he was at the pool year after year waiting for the angel, he could have been discouraged because he had no one. Didn't he have family and friends to help him? Jesus asked why was he just sitting there his response was I have no man. Meaning I have no one my family and friends have deserted me. How desperate was he I'm convinced he must have been pretty desperate.

Taking a look at another picture who spends 13 years in jail for a crime he did not commit and does not get discouraged. Joseph was away from civilization for 13 years all he had were his dreams. He must have thought to himself are these dreams ever going to come true? Even the people he helped get out of prison forgot him when they got out. What an unfair situation. He could have gotten angry or jealous or even envious however he remained there until his season of change came. What do you do when all you have is your dreams and it seems

they are never going to come to pass. He was so hated by his family they wanted him dead only the mercies of God kept him. So then how does one produce good fruits I might ask? You might be inviting an individual to church for years and at first they want to have nothing to do with God. But one plants one waters and God gives the increase maybe this individual may not go with you but a situation may come up in their lives when finally they give their heart to the Lord.

People do not realize that the choices that they make on earth seals where they

end up after death. There was a rich man called diavese and a beggar called Lazarus. The rich man ate scrumptiously while Lazarus ate the crumbs off the rich mans table. He died and opened his eyes in hell while Lazarus died and went into the busom of Abraham. Diavese was in so much torment that he had one request ask Lazarus for a drop of water to ease the torment of the hellfire he was told that there is a gulf between them and they are separated for eternity. He asked them to warn his brothers not to come to this place. The answer was, if they did

not believe the prophets that were sent why would they believe him.

There are many outcastes that Jesus visited the lepers who were outcasts whenever they went any where near to the town LEPER was called out and they had to leave because no one would associate with them they said to themselves why sit we here until we die if we go into town we will be killed and if we stay here we will die of hunger so they took the only chance they had and went into town and when they went the

town was empty and they had food to sustain them.

Jesus also had a moment of crisis when all forsaken him. In his moment of crisis he was sweat drops of blood while he was forsaken by his disciples. The heart is willing but the flesh is weak.

The woman at the well was also another person Jesus made a special trip to see. He told her how many husbands she had and that the one she was with now was not her own.

The woman who anointed Jesus's feet with the expensive perfume was shunned because Jesus's disciples said doesn't He know what manner of woman this is.

Isn't it wonderful that it's not the person who everyone see as respectful that Jesus puts on a pedestal. However He sits high and looks low. He respects the humble and resists the proud. Seven things doth the Lord hate approved good and seventh is an abomination, those who sew discord amongst the brethren.

God is a God of compassion, he looked on the multitude and had compassion. He had compassion on many people, if you are harsh with no compassion I don't know who you're God is.

I give God thanks for having shoes on my feet because I remember years ago in the winter when it snowed the bottom of my boots were so tattered my feet were so frost bitten it was like torture. God has brought me a long way, this is why I can be compassionate to others it's because I've been there. I walked in their shoes. I had to be in school from 8 am - 12

pm and worked from 1 pm to midnight around the clock so I know what hard work is all about. It has not been easy but I learned to be grateful.

You have to be like Enoch Enoch walked with the Lord until he was translated. He pleased the Lord so much he did not see death. Elijah was carried into Heaven by chariots of fire he did not have to taste death.

As I end this book if anyone has reads this book and decides they would like to give Jesus a try to work in their lives simply pray this pray. Dear Lord please

forgive me for my sins. I confess you with my mouth and receive you in my heart as my Lord and Savior Jesus Christ.

Printed in the United States
By Bookmasters